SELECTED POEMS

OF

ANDREI VOZNESENSKY

SELECTED POEMS

OF

ANDREI VOZNESENSKY

Translated and with an Introduction by

Anselm Hollo

GROVE PRESS, INC.   NEW YORK

CONTENTS

SELECTED POEMS

OF

ANDREI VOZNESENSKY

ANDREI VOZNESENSKY

An Introduction

Since 1958, when his first verses were published in *Literaturnaya Gazeta*, Andrei Voznesensky has steadily made his way into the forefront of contemporary Russian literature: he is, undoubtedly, the most inventive and original representative of the Russian "new wave"—the "thaw," etc.; but it would be doing him great injustice to leave it at that, to see his importance solely in terms of the cultural environment of his own country and society. The impressive and vital aspect of his poetry does not consist of reactions against or within such a framework, but of an awareness, a vision of man's mind today, at this point of *human*—not political, Communist, or capitalist—history. In his own words: "The basic problem of contemporary literature: to look deep into the human mind, right inside the brain!" The most personal, unique quality of Voznesensky is just that: the accuracy and freshness with which the sudden shifts and gestures of the mind are caught, and made over into words—like trajectory photographs of fireflies in the dark.

While still a student at the Moscow Institute of Architecture, Andrei Voznesensky was a frequent visitor at the home of Boris Pasternak. "I used to see a lot of him until one day when he said: 'Andrei, if I had written these poems, I would include them unhesitatingly in my next book.' Oddly enough, I wasn't flattered. It gave me a jolt. I didn't want to be a mere imitator. For two years I returned to my architectural studies. But then I started writing poetry again, and when I brought my new batch to Pasternak, he said: 'Yes, this is no longer Pasternak, this is Voznesensky, a poet in his own right.' Nobody's opinion mattered to me so much as Pasternak's. I felt I had now 'made it.'"

Since then Voznesensky, now twenty-nine years old, has published three books of poems, all of them what Soviet critics like to call "pure poetry"—that is to say, scarcely ever political or polemical in the manner of his friend and contemporary Yevgeni Yevtushenko. Thus it is an encouraging and even miraculous fact that his popularity among young Russians is, today, even greater than Yevtushenko's: however cynically reassuring it may be to think that the general popularity of poetry readings in Moscow and elsewhere in the Soviet Union is mostly due to crypto-politics and the lack of other, or more diversified, audio-visual entertainment (like TV serials?), the fact of a genuine audience of at least 50,000 people—this, the number of copies printed of Voznesensky's last book, *The Three-Cornered Pear*—for structurally complex, personal, at times even idiosyncratic poems, is bound to make one, as they say, think. . . . Voznesensky himself says these readers are "above all our young technical intelligentsia: there are millions of them in Russia now. Many of them work on enormously complicated machines—and they want poetry to be complicated, too. They have no use for rhymed editorials. . . . We're overstuffed with rhymes: all fifth-form pupils make up wonderful rhymes. Our poetry's future lies in association, metaphors reflecting the inter-

10

dependence of phenomena, their mutual transformation." And: "As a matter of fact, it is not a question of 'form' at all: the form must be clear, at best exciting and full of the most profound ideas—like the sky, in which only radar can detect the presence of a plane."

As these quotes show, Voznesensky's attitude toward technology (as well as the technicians' attitude toward him) differs greatly from most Western poets' stance vis-à-vis The Machine and its Men. But anyone eager to plaster the clichés of "Futurist . . . 20's . . . etc." onto Voznesensky should, I think, ask himself whether this acceptance of the tools and the artificial surroundings of modern man, an un-prejudiced and even—if the facts seem to warrant it—en-thusiastic way of looking at them, is not a good deal more "advanced" and useful than the perennial fabrication of metaphors of destruction and doom out of these manifesta-tions of technology? Perhaps the point—or at least one point, today—about the "dark Satanic mills" is that not they, but the "Satanic" should, and what's more, *could* be abolished. . . .

The young woman referred and spoken to in Voznesen-sky's two poems "Who Are You?" and "Where Are You?" stands for Russian youth in the present period of transition, for its doubts, quandaries, general feeling of "lostness"—but also for its hope and belief that it will be possible to find a new and clearer way of life, of which a "humanized tech-nology" would be an essential part. "Not the tool, but who wields it. . . ."

Rublyov, the old Russian icon painter; Goya; Gauguin; Miró—this eclectic roll-call of painters is heard in Voznesen-sky's poems, and a sense of freedom and liberation in the worlds of shapes and color, combined with the "inward vision" of a Paul Klee, will be found in them. Also, indica-tions of influences by the great classics of modern European

11

poetry, Apollinaire with his Cubist mind-jumps and juxta-
positions, Mayakovsky, Pasternak, and Federico Garcia
Lorca: the visionary clarity and sharpness of his images. . . .
To him, Voznesensky pays moving homage, in "Lover of
Lorca": this section of prose gives greater insight into the
mind that is Andrei Voznesensky than any amount of analyt-
ical or descriptive wordage could, and I would like to end
this introductory note by quoting a paragraph from it here:
"Poetry always means revolution. The hypocrite jailers of
the New Inquisition recognized it in the songs of Lorca: he
was all freedom inside, abandon and wildness. A tulip, growing at the foot of a concrete bulwark: it is like a shout of
rebellion."

A tulip,
      Andrei—
it is late,
      here in my London room . . .
black window:
      but closing my eyes
I created this tulip
      for you—
    the horns
  of Jericho stood
      no taller
    against the sky—
against the sky! Yes
   I can see
      no wall
—only
    the tulip
we know.

Anselm Hollo
London, August 1963

THE LILAC TREE, "MOSCOW—WARSAW"

For R. Gamzatov

10.3.61

The lilac tree is taking leave,
The lilac tree is like a track of ski
Like a poodle, licking my cheeks!
The lilac tree has a tear-streaked face,
The lilac tree is a Czar's daughter
The lilac tree glows like acetylene!
Rassul Gamzatov glowers like a bison bull.
Rassul Gamzatov said, "Take it away!"

11.3.61

Rassul feels weak now. Rassul can't sleep.
In the train compartment the lilac tree is trembling
Like a girl in a cold bath. How scared it is!
Down below
        the train-wheels, rumbling,
                no black soil at all.

And yet, perhaps it is more "beautiful" to bloom in May. . . .
My double, my magic, lilac tree, lilac tree

13

Lilac tree, kindred spirit!
                    Among all its relations
It alone flowers in this third dimension of speed!

A hundred wild goats—
                    only one gazelle.
A hundred penny-whistles—
                    a single flute.
To bloom in a garden, before one's time.
There are a hundred lilac trees—
                         I love only this one!
Its nocturnal clusters give off a voluptuous rustling sound
Like microphones made out of German silver.
My God, what a tree ...
                    And not a head
                         without a migraine.
The lilac tree stands like a hundred military honors.

12.3.61

The Customs Officer jumps: "A live one? A tree?"
The Customs Officer groaned, forgetting the rules.
O for the sense of wonder, the seventh sense!
A green chandelier, it circumnavigates the planet
Whistling through all the spaces between villages and stars—
The lilac tree, drawing its bill!
And smiling
          at the soil, at the grass, at the laws. ...

P.S.
I get a letter: "The lilac tree has died."

14

THE BIG FIRE AT THE
ARCHITECTURAL COLLEGE

There's a fire
In the Architectural!
Those halls!
Those drawings all
On fire! like letters of amnesty
On fire! on fire!

Like a red-ass gorilla
Up there on the sleepy façade—
The window,
Uncoiling, roaring
To fight—to open
On fire!

We've been studying
For our finals, yes
It's time to defend our thesis!
My pronouncements already crackling
In the sealed
Safe—

Like a huge bottle
Of kerosene—
Five summers, five winters
Swoosh up in flames
O my sweet Karen,
O we're on fire!
The little notes
For cheating at tests, the parties
All gone, going-gone, up up
In these flames—
There you stand, pink
                    in the blueberry patch—
Good-bye, good-bye!

Farewell Architecture!
Farewell in flames
You cowsheds with little Cupids
You Savings Banks in baroque!
O youth o Phoenix

O stupid, on fire
Is your final certificate!
O youth you're waggling your ass
In a red skirt, O youth
You're wagging your tongue—

Farewell, time of boundary
Measurements! This is life
—moving one from one burning lot
To another—we're all
On fire, you live—
                    you're on fire!

What winches, what mainstays
Will be born in this fire—
To run across
The sheets of Watman's Paper
Like the first tracks
Of ski?
But tomorrow, twittering
Like an evil bird
And angrier than a hornet
The pair of compasses will be found
In a handful of ashes, and
Sting. . . .

Everything's burnt down now,
Good.
        Everybody
Draw a real deep breath.
Everything over?
                Everything's started!
Now, let's go see
That movie.

THE RUBLYOV HIGHROAD

The motor scooters are streaming past the sanatorium
The handlebar lovers,
                    looking like Rublyov angels.
Dazzling white frescoes of Annunciation
                              their women,
Shining like wings
                grown out of their shoulders.
Their skirts
          in the wind
                    in flying-back folds—
Come, pierce me with your white wings!
                              Will I fly?
Disappear as a falcon?
                    Or stone?
                         O eyes.
                    Skies. Red forests.

Andrey Rublyov, 1370-1430, a priest, the greatest Russian icon painter.
(*Tr. note.*)

SEASON OF WATERMELONS

Moscow is flooded with watermelons!
  Boundless freedom pervades the city.
    The market-women full of excitement and power!

Tents. Noise. The girls' bright headscarves.
  Laughter. Clink of coins, and knives
    carving fat insolent slices.

    —You take that one, mister, won't regret it!
    Melons melons, who wants watermelons?
    Any size or slice you like, we're here to please!—

As juicy and tempting seem the red visors of the militia,
  the wheels of the scooters standing by the wall—
    the September air tastes fresh and melony,

And as happily wildly as those melons at the gates
  the earth is turning—good luck!
    to its meridians and latitudes.

DIVAGATION ABOUT MYSELF

J.-P. Sartre

I am a family, a spectrum:
There are seven of "me" inside me,
Unbearable,
Like seven beasts—
   and the bluest of these
               keeps whistling through its pipe!
But when Spring comes,
        dreams come:
               that I'm—
      the eighth.

FOGGY STREET

A fogbound suburb, like a fat
Cock-pigeon.
Like anchor-buoys
The militiamen.
              Foggy weather.
What century is it? What era?
Everything's shattered, delirious.
The people, as if
             they'd been taken apart.

I roam through the streets
Or rather, struggle through cottonwool.
Noses. Small headlights. . . . Vizors. Everything double.
Your galoshes, sir. You've got the right head, I trust?

That is
            the way she is. Soon as her lips leave mine
She is at least two, and alive, yet not mine anymore—
A widow: a moment ago
             she was yours, and now: a stranger.

   I brush past people, lampposts. . . . Venus?
No, an ice-cream vendor. Friends?
O they are hothouse flowers. . . . And you?

You just stand there, pinching your earlobes,
All alone, in that enormous cape.
  And what is that? A mustache?!
  And hoarfrost in that hairy old ear!

Stumble on, fight and live through the fog,
          and you'll never **know**
Whose cheek you are touching—Ouch! Murk, murk—
  No one can hear you shout. . . .
  How good it is
     when the day
       breaks clear!

WHO ARE YOU?

What are we: poker chips or great men?
Cells of genius in the blood of this planet—
Indivisible: no "builders," no "poets"
"Pygmies"—or hipsters, passing the word:

Whatever we do, the smallpox of time won't get us!
"Who are you?"—it is like a punch in the face,
All of a sudden: sucked forward, we go
The cinders are flying back from our heels.

Who are you, who are you? Then, all of a sudden?
Aphrodite is itching to cast off her cloak. . . .
Starlings scurry to mate with strong crows—
Architects! open your mouths, to build a new poem.

And the poet-girls, running, running, the thaw in their palms
Toward the trembling black grove. . . .
But you?
            For months on end you've been aiming at stars
& tramping the roads. You finished your school
You cut off your tresses, became a salesgirl and gave that up.
And again & again, repetitiously, like children's games . . .
I see you
            there, surrounded by posters and slogans
A lost, tiny woman, and out of breath. . . .

Who are you? who? as sadly you stare at the books
Into the windows—but who, who are you there?
Or bending, over a microscope, or likewise over
The pupils, immobile, of those men's eyes. . . .

But I am with you, lost with you, Vera, Vega!
Even I am impossible, among the avalanches of white—
As impossible to track down as the Snowman
In the great Himalayas.

WHERE ARE YOU?

You live with your aunt.
She loves *canzoni*.
She sneezes.
She likes to wear masculine
Underwear.
O we hate her,
The damned old hag. . . .

O we're good friends with the old couch.
As one is friends with a peaceably minded bear.
It keeps us warm, like a breast in a palm
And there's this smell
Of beehives,
Beehives among the trees

    —but in Susdal it's Easter!
    but in Susdal there are great crowds
    there is laughter, there are wheeling
    swarms of crows—

Through my cheek you are telling me your childhood
Whispering, of a child in that village, of suns
And horses, and beehives, resplendent like icons.
That sheen of honey is still on your hair. . . .

I live in Russia—surrounded by snow and Saints.

YOU SIT THERE

You sit there, big with child and pale.
There have been changes made.
You sit there, tugging at your skirt and
Wanting to cry.

Yes. What on earth
Do they get out of it? Women
Falling, letting us enter as they fall
Upon us—then, later, running to see us
Go by at the crossing, then, later, staying
Staying, when the last carriage has passed.

How you ran, after that train.
Staring at windows blurred into streaks of black glass.
Khabarovsk, Lyuberetzk
Express trains, mail trains, all go
Rumbling by.

And from Moscow to Ash'khabad
—stricken: to the point of muteness
Stone-like, these women stand
Offering their big bellies to the moon.
And, as it is turning toward the light
In its nightly existence, unlived,

How well it can understand them,
That planet
Heavy with an enormous pale belly. . . .

FIRST ICE

In the phone booth, a girl
    cold in her shivery coat,
all tears, her face a
    chaos of smudgy make-up.
She tries to blow warmth
    into her paper-thin palms.
Her fingers—small lumps of ice.
    Yes, earrings. But now
she has to go back, alone,
    down the frozen street.

    First ice. First ice.
First ice of cold
    clichés on the telephone.
The frozen tracks
    shimmering on her cheeks.
First ice of humiliation.

GOYA

I am Goya: my eyes are destroyed
by enemy beaks.
    Shell-holes stare from the naked field.

I am misery,

    the Voice of War
the voice of charred cities' timber
on the snow of the year
    Forty-one.

I am the old woman's throat
who was hung, whose body sang like a bell
over the naked townsquare. . . .

I am Goya
Grapes of Wrath! Dust
I am, raised by the barrage in the West.
    Dust of the intruder . . .

And bright stars

were hammered in the memorial sky

like nails.

Yes, I
am Goya.

FIRST DEDICATION FOR "THE MASTERS"

The bells, the ringers of bells,
The tolling, the tolling . . .
    for you,
Artists
       of all times!

For you, Michelangelo
Barma, Dante!
You who were charred
Alive by the lightning
Of your gifts.

Your hammer,
Not chipping
            at columns
And statues,
          struck
At crowns, struck them down!
And shook
       the thrones.

The artist, a first-born,
Is always a hero
Among his people.
What moves him is
The spirit of change,
He is a vessel
Of constant rebellion.
They walled you in,
They burned you at the stake.
Monks,
        dancing like ants
On your bones.

But your art rose again
From executions and torture,
Striking the stones
Of the Moabites
Like flint.

The bleeding
Calluses on your hands.
The ashes, the sweat.
And the muse, like Zoë
Led to the scaffold.

But there is no serum
Against her
            holy words—
Makers,
        fighters,
Yours
      is the glory.

EDUARDO DE FILIPPO

His face reminds you of those austere, weather-beaten early Renaissance buildings. We are talking about the "Contemporary" Theater, about Hemingway and Pasolini. Suddenly a smile, a strangely embarrassed smile appears on his crudely stone-carved lips: —I should really go back now, I have these engagements. . . . But I want to be in Moscow on May Day!

I return the smile: smiles are untranslatable. We had just visited the studio of a Moscow artist. The faces of eleventh-century Novgorod woodcuts stared at us from the walls, in strange harmony with the modern furnishings of the room and with the sounds of the railroad tracks below the window.

I stepped out onto the balcony. The city was asleep, no light in the windows of the house opposite. I could feel the strong light of the klieg lamp inside striking my back through the open balcony door.

My enormous, hyperbolical shadow flattened itself on the house opposite as if on a screen, covering, engulfing countless windows. Behind those windows, behind the walls, their openings, I knew there were whole mountains of lives: people sleeping, people making love with upturned faces, people thinking, pondering something all their own. A few windows were open. My shadow entered them like the smell of tobacco smoke and lilac bloom at night, my shadow united them all.

There I was, watching this huge, ghostly shape, outside and apart from myself. Under its shaggy rule there were hundreds of lives. "Yes, that is art," I remember thinking, "that is the way men are united by it. . . ."

Below me, Moscow was floating. Breathing, dissolving into mists.

POEM

Frost, laughter, horses trotting,
Dogs barking. And we have been working like all hell—
But tonight we'll cut loose! Cut loose! Up
                          their skirts!
Hey-ho, in the blue-glazed yet fiery sleds—
The brass spires, gleaming:
                  poached eggs on the snow plains.
Come on, mouth
            to mouth! Past fairs
With gloriously painted eggs and jugs and jars,
Through this Russia of cathedrals and sable,
Thrugh Russia, torn and tattered—
                    hey—let's go!
Tomorrow will be
            another day, of work, but dazzling and new.
O my dear carpenters,
              plane your boards to build the new cities!
   Cities? Or, perhaps
               coffins?

BALLAD OF THE YEAR '41

The piano disappeared into the quarry,
It was dragged down to the firewood store:
Frozen vats and boxes of chaff.
Now it was waiting
                    for the breaker's ax.

It had no feet, it was a black box,
Lay on its belly, droned
Quietly, breathing, a black armadillo
In this deep, man-made den.

His swollen fingers reddened again:
On the left hand: two, on the right hand: five...
He knelt, to reach the fingerboard.
Seven fingers, all he had left, the one-time master.
Frozen and stiff, they sloughed their cold skin like the peel
Comes off a steaming potato. But then, a continuous
Flame: they played ... gods, beauty ...

Everything, anything ever played on that box
Had been an enormous lie! Reflections
Of candelabra and pillars ...

I hear the steel of that piano roaring inside me.
I lie in the quarry, and I am huge like a piano
Reflecting the shiny black dust of the walls:
Human shapes. Hunger. Flesh glowing at the stake.
As if waiting for crowning glories I wait
For the breaker's ax!

No secret, my mission,
    true to my fate
I'll be a high music,
    warmth and bread, for men.

BALLAD OF THE PARABOLA

Fate flies
          like a rocket, on a parabolic curve—
Mostly in darkness, but sometimes—
                                        it's a rainbow.
Consider the fiery-haired painter Gauguin:
Bohemian, yes, used to be a stockbroker. . . .
To get from Montmartre to the Louvre he flew
A detour:
          Java, Sumatra!
The madness of money
                    he left behind, and the cackle of women,
The hot sticky air of Academies,
                              he defied
                                        gravity.
The high priests sneered by their tankards:
     "The straight line is shorter, the parabola steep—
     is it not better to copy the groves
                                        of Paradise?"
But he, a roaring rocket flew
Through the wind that was cutting off coats' tails and ears
Not making the Louvre
                         through the big portals—
But on a furious parabola, crashing through
                                        the ceiling!

36

Lives move into truth
                    so variously brave:
For the worm—it's a crack, for a man—a parabola.
There was a girl next door, we studied, passed exams
    together.
But where did it get me! The devil lured me away
To stare at the ornate, ambiguous stars of Tiflis!
Forgive me
            this useless parabola.
Cold, thin shoulders under your black Sunday dress . . . God,
What a sound you made in the darkness
                            up there:
Straight and firm like the aerial whip of a radio transmitter
While I am still flying, flying,
                        then landing on earth
There comes a terrestrial, frozen signal from you!
How hard it is to remember this journey.
Sweeping aside all canons, all prognostications, paragraphs
Art, love and history follow the parabolic
Trajectory.
                His rubber boots, drowning
                                in Siberian spring. . . .
Maybe the straight line
Is shorter?

BALLAD OF THE .

A ballad? About the full stop? The deadly . ?
O fools! Have you forgotten Pushkin's bullet?
Forgotten the winds whistling through the holes
Of that fine clarinet—
The perforated heads of our
Great poets.

Piercing the walls of arrogance, bestiality,
The trajectory of that bullet hits—
                              their offspring!
There was no . any more. It was a beginning.

Into the earth we depart
Through the gates of its railway station:
The full stop
              at the end of the tunnel
                              is black,
Like the snout of a gun.
Where *does* it stop? Immortality? The Unknown?

No death. No full stop, either. But the bullet-drawn line—
A second projection of the same horizontal.
According to calculations, they say, the full stop is
                              nonexistent in nature.
So we'll be immortal all right.
                    Precisely that.

CROWNS AND ROOTS

To the memory of L. N. Tolstoy

They were carrying him away—
But not to bury him:
They were carrying him away
To a coronation.

Grayer than granite,
Yet gleaming like bronze, and smoking
    like a locomotive this artist lived,
    a tousled life. . . . To him, shovels
    were more divine
                than the lights lit
                    in front of icons.

His lilac tree withered. . . .
At the time of falling stars
His back was steaming with sweat,
A great loaf
            in the oven.

Now his house
Is a yawn of emptiness. . . .
Desolate floors,
                no one enters
                    the dining room.
In Russia
            not a soul.

The artists take leave,
Bareheaded, enter
The humming fields and forests
Of birch and oak, like a church.

Their escape is their victory.
Their departure
                    a sunrise,
On meadow-glens, planets
Gilded with tinsel.

The forests are losing
                    their leafy crowns.
But under the soil,
                    the roots are
Twisting and turning:
                        five
                            gnarled fingers.

AT NIGHT

I have been exiled into myself.
I am—Mikhailovskoye.
My pine trees are burning.

In my face, dimmed like a mirror
Elk and white ptarmigan move.

The world is in the river and in me
And still somewhere else,
Outside.

Three red suns, burning.
Three groves, trembling, three glasses

Three women fading into one another
Like *matrjeshki*-dolls—
Onionwise.

One of them loves me, laughs.
Another, inside her, twitters like a bird.

But the third one,
She crawls away in a corner
Like a lump of coal.

She won't forgive me.
She lusts for revenge.

Her face shines into my eyes
From the bottom of a well:
A ring.

Mikhailovskoye: Pushkin was banished there. (*Tr. note.*)

TAIGA

Your teeth are brave.
They smile like a knife.
Your golden eyes,
They buzz like bees!

We go out of the hut,
The tall grass to our ears.
You prophesy reprimands
From friends and relations.

But you're not a nun,
Though there be hermit huts . . .
The furry bees go,
Bending down flowers.

I don't know the taiga.
I don't know the family.
I only know your eyes.
Your teeth I know.

The dew in the sunflowers'
Buddhist bowls.
How sweet it tastes
On the ear lobes of violets!

Inside each drop
You, naked, reflected
Woman of Lilliput
Bending the petals.

You, living water
On lips and leaves.
You, giving yourself
To the last drop—to the taiga.

BICYCLES

For V. Bokov

The bicycles lie
In the woods, in the dew.
    Between the birch trees
    The highroad gleams.

They fell, fell down
Mudguard to mudguard,
    Handlebar to handlebar
    Pedal to pedal.

And you can't
Wake them up!
    Petrified monsters,
    Their chains entwined.

Huge and surprised
They stare at the sky.
    Above them, green dusk
    Resin, and bumblebees.

In the luxurious
Rustling of camomile, peppermint
    Leaves they lie. Forgotten,
    Asleep. Asleep.

45

ON THE BANKS OF THE YENISSEI

For W. Syakin

In summer he works at logging, in the wintertime he drives around with the huskies. And a ladies' man, if ever there was one.

Just now, he sits there polishing a small tin plate, telling us about his journey with a schoolmistress whom he had been taking up North. . . .

—And then the blizzard hit us! So what can a man do? Only thing there is to do when those things start blowing, is get into your sleeping-bag, cover yourself up and wait till it's over. But we had *only one sleeping-bag* between us—so, what can a man do? Well. We had to wait for it to blow over, all of three days and three nights!

His words are drowned in laughter: don't we know, only too well, what sort of "waiting" that was. . . . He looks around, confusion in his eyes:

—What you staring at—you all nuts or something? I didn't even touch her—how could I, having dragged her into this, this catastrophe—!

He goes on cursing us for a long while. Then he gets up, lopes to the door, out onto the porch. Stands there, listening to the moon.

Well, there's a poem for you.

B. AKHMADULINA

This girl
        was given a spark,
Not a piece of candy—
                a spark:
To look for things, and to dare
To have the courage
            of a goddess.

You can light a heart with it
Or a stove, or set
The earth on fire
         and burn it
              to hell!

The spark dies away
          in the tip
             of her cigarette
And she smiles,
        cunningly.

Bella Akhmadulina, well-known young Russian poetess of Voznesensky's own generation, an ex-wife of Yevgeni Yevtushenko. (*Tr. note.*)

47

BIRCH TREES IN GEORGIA

By the wanton brook,
By the glazed mountains—
    birch trees in Inguri!
    Birch trees
           in Inguri!
Like temple portals
    columns, transparent
        these trees stand.
It is like a homecoming
    as I enter the grove,
        spreading my arms
    flinging myself on the ground
        to lie there until
            night falls.
Dusk, thickening above me, white
    the tree-trunks wave and mingle
        above me, become transparent.
As light, as straight
    on their circular platform
        the floodlights stand,
    a guard of honor
        in the sky
            above Moscow.
I love their weightlessness,
    high harmony: against this whiteness
        I can test my conscience.

FROM THE WINDOW OF A PLANE

In the world of friends
    where travel is slower
what are you doing,
    in the world
of rain?
    With whom are you sharing
a tangerine?
    Or tearing
up notes for a test
    to be taken again?

    You, pretty witch
and Merciless Lady
    —still tossing that mane?
Raising your eyebrows . . .
    Or running,
like hammers
    inside a piano
down past the railings,
    the grove of pillars. . . .
O my beautiful lady
are you still tossing
    that charm around?
Or is it chilled feet

            crossing & crossing
a cold dark room
            —passing & passing
the telephone
            in a zone of gloom
the receiver black
            heavy, a dumbell. . . .

            Yes I have heard
you are married,
            and I am about
to forget you.
            Why is it then
that I see you again
            cold in that world below,
rushing by
            in the soft sweet rain
that is freezing
            the wing, you come
to mind's eye?

PARTY

A great drunken crowd
Round the table.
But suddenly
Two are
                missing! Where are they?
                        Maybe the wind—?
In the midst of all
Serious drinking: two empty chairs,
Two paralyzed knives.
                        And a moment ago
They were lifting their beakers—
Then, nothing.
                    Not here, those two.
Like snow in the sun. . . .
                            Go ahead,
Look for them,
                whistle and call!
They got away,
                not caring
A damn
        for overcoats
                        and decorum.
Ran away like the wine
Hums out of the bottle!

Thus go rivers
               speeding past their banks,
Thus clouds go,
               the young from the old,
In Spring
        the new shoots
                  from old trunks.
The party is roaring on.
But these two, their
               courage, two
Overturned chairs—
            has taken
                  our breath away.

A NEW YEAR'S LETTER

A. L.

These guests! heavy
    like hot-water bottles—
all in a row
    on their napkins
their hands lie, red
    like lobsters
on a plate. . . .
    And you! lost
among these enormous
    bowls, cooling
your cheek
    on a wine glass—
off comes
    your shawl,
you're burning! "It's so
    hot in here—"
But back at my place
    the window's
wide open, on the tall
    city, as onto
a garden—and the snow
    smelling like

apples, yellow
    Antonovka apples
its flakes
    suspended
in air.
    They don't move
they don't fall
    they're waiting,
weightless, static,
    observant
like small icon
    lamps, or tobacco
plants in summer:
    but they'll swing
in small arcs
    when touched
by a little foot
    in a smart Polish boot . . .
and the snow
and the smell of apples.

LOVER OF LORCA

I love Lorca. I love his name, hovering lightly like a boat, humming like the gallery in a theater, vibrating with the sensitivity of the moon-disk of a radio relay station; smelling as bitter and intense as orange rind. . . .

Lorca!

He was a rambler, a comedian, a rambler in dreams, a painter. De Falla says Lorca's musical gifts were equal to his talent as a poet.

I never saw him. I was born too late. I meet him every day.

When I see the two brightly burnished moons, one in the river, the other in the sky—I want to cry out, to one of Lorca's boys: "It is midnight, let the cymbals clash!" When I hear someone say, "Cordoba," I feel I know them: the two misty Cordobas, the town and its buildings and the other, which is water lilies at nightfall. . . . I know their heart, vulnerable and transparent like "silk, wafted by the ray of light, by weightlessly ringing bells." I know nothing more accurate in its psychology than his "Faithless Woman": that purity and emotion, shining like mother-of-pearl! And I love to listen, when in his ballads

> Gypsies and seraphs
> Play the accordion . . .

Franco's men killed him on the 18th of August, 1936. The murderers. They try to explain it away as some kind of accident—all these "accidents!" Pushkin, a misunderstanding? Lermontov, a mistake?!

———————

Poetry always means revolution. The hypocrite jailers of the New Inquisition recognized it in the songs of Lorca: he was all freedom inside, abandon and wildness. A tulip, growing at the foot of a concrete bulwark: it is like a shout of rebellion.

Marx said that poets are in need of much tenderness: what tenderness is it that tears a poet's heart to shreds in the thickets of barbed wire? When I think of this tragic road, ending in destruction, I am also reminded of Eluard: he was poisoned by gas in the First World War—the choking poet, a symbolic figure. How can you sing, when you cannot even breathe?

Lorca's voice, hoarse and wrathful:

> This is not hell, this is a road.
> This is not death, this is a fruiterer's store.
> I can see unfathomable worlds in the broken paw
> Of a kitten, crushed by your shiny automobiles.

———————

Those wildly sprouting metaphors of Lorca!

> Like the measured tolling of bells
> Is the bulls' heavy tread:
> From birth their souls have yearned for death,
> They despise the yoke, remembering two wings
> That used to grow out of their flanks, and beat.

The metaphor is the engine of a poem. The twentieth century is a century of enormous change, of metamorphoses. What, today, is a pine tree? Perlon? Or fiberglass for rockets? At night, my shaggy sweater dreams of Siberian firs, of the rustling needles on the hairy branches of its ancestors. . . .

Lorca, associations: in his poetry the sky gleams like "the croup of a black mare." A man leans out of the window, and the wind comes and cuts his head off, like the triangular blade of a guillotine.

Objects become aware of their relations, start calling out to each other. The same happens in Picasso's work—certainly in the drawings he has made for Eluard's poetry: the outline of a woman's face blends into the oval shape of a dove, her eyebrows bloom out into palm leaves, and what do we see there? Her hair? or the wings of a dove?

I have seen Lorca's paintings, from them you get the same sense of Gypsy-Spanish grace and nobility as in his ballads. But in his poems the painter's eye goes wild: he loves the local—how penetrating the green in his "Sleepwalker's Romance":

> I love you, clad in green.
> The wind, also, is green.
> And the leaves.
> A ship on the green sea, and a horse
> On the wooded skyline. Green
> Is the hair, the body,
> Cooler than silver
>   the eyes . . .
> O let me go, let me rise and go
> To the green corral of the moon!

With what precision that moonlight has been transformed into green—into an "emerald," one might say! But in "The Murder of Antonito el Camborio" red is the dominant color.

Heavy gold gleams in the "Four Yellow Ballads." And the most terrifying and overwhelming coloration of black appears in the "Romance of the Guardia Civil":

> The black horses of the Guardia Civil
> Are shod with black irons.
> Above their black capes,
> Waxed inkblots shine.

He keeps repeating this, the blackness, "black, black," and they begin to black out the sky in your eyes, these gendarmes. It is their rightful symbol.

> The black Guardia Civil goes at a gallop,
> Covers the roadside with funeral pyres,
> Burning poetry at the stake
> It stands, naked and beautiful.
>
> A rose of the Camborios falls
> On the threshold, with a groan:
> In front of her, on a platter lie
> Her mutilated breasts.
>
> The other young women run,
> They run away, their black tresses
> Flapping in the wind, the air
> Now flowers with bullets—black roses.

Poetry is first of all a miracle. A miracle of emotion, of tone and of a "something" without which you cannot even begin to imagine a work of art. It is inexplicable. People lacking the inner ear for this music did not understand Lorca: woe unto the sad ears of these eunuchs who have posted themselves on the outskirts of literature. . . .

Poems tend to magnify the emotions of their readers, their listeners. If there is nothing there, to magnify, even poetry is powerless!

How could one paraphrase the magic of these lines:

> Tell the ladies that I have died,
> Mother, send out blue telegrams
> From the South to the North!

I grieve for Lorca.

I grieve for his music. It had the scent of lemons: light and bitterness.

———

And yet another encounter with Lorca:

There are about half-a-million Poles in Chicago, and it so happened that I read my poem about the "Lilac Tree" there: it is a balladesque poem, about a footloose, infatuated little lilac tree that left home and hit the road. . . .

The lunar rectangle of the TV screen lights this little room. They've switched off the sound, instead of a lamp there is only the lilac-tinted screen with mute shadows floating across it. In this light a woman, sitting on the couch. She is Polish. She sits there, her legs tucked up under her. Her parents emigrated to Argentina before the war. She looks restless and lost. Against the lilac gloom she looks like a lilac tree herself, with her stooping, tremulous shoulders, her bluish hair, the gray, strange, veiled eyes: yes, she is a lilac tree, shimmering and lost—I find myself reading about her, her life, without really understanding it myself.

What does she live by? What moves in her soul? Where the straw she is grasping at in this void, this alien world?

Instead of replying to my question she raises her face and starts reading out, no, reciting, almost singing a poem, herself. A transformation! Her thin, small voice rings out clear, and she looks happy now—a creature of the dawn.

—That was by Lorca, she then says, answering my astonished stare. . . .

—Lark? I say, misunderstanding. . . .

—Yes, the lark, she laughs: —He is my great joy, I don't know what I'd do without him. The Lark . . . Lorca.

They killed him, on the 18th of August, 1936.

Lorca's teachings are not to be found only in his songs, in his life: his annihilation also is an important lesson. Art and its makers are still being murdered. Only in Spain? As I am writing this, the jailers of Siqueiros are—maybe—taking him for his daily walk round the courtyard. . . .

Twenty-five years ago they killed Lorca.

(FROM A NOTEBOOK)

—three nights in a row I roam through Greenwich Village, the "picturesque" and senseless *quartier* of Bohemian New York. The bearded sphinx of the Beat confronts me with endless riddles. Like the inscription above a brightly lit café entrance: "Wha?"! What is "Wha?" Somebody says—"Wha" is the outcry of the modern soul. . . . All right, let's hear it.

All gloom and mystique, in the little cellar downstairs. Waterpipes curl across the low ceiling. Someone is reading rhythmical prose-cum-jazz. A sleepy wildman who looks like a stray from a fancy-dress ball in his torn *khiton* receives the visitors at the door. His hairy soul is steaming out of the rents and holes of that jersey: "Wha?"

Épater le bourgeois? Is that it? Or is it just fashionable exoticism? . . .

———

My sketches cannot give a fair impression of this country, America: they are like snapshots taken in a lift that is speeding from one floor to the other.

Architecture?

I loved the Guggenheim Museum, the swan song of Frank Lloyd Wright who was a genius. Imagine a dazzling, elastic spiral as a building, curving skyward—and inside, moving down along the walls and curves, on a gentle slope, you can see the paintings, in a restful, downward motion.

Talents are born in two's. The arts are communicating vessels; there are *doppelgänger* in the arts. This is easiest to realize when looking at paintings. Zabolotski's purity and naïveté communicate with the primitive vision of Henri Rousseau; Picasso's extravagant meals-in-paint tell you more about Lorca than a thousand translations. But the optimistic tunes of A. A. Prokofyev associate themselves with Shishkin, and with the woodwork on a roof-ridge of a *kolkhoz* club-house.

Something stronger than mere "interest" nails me down for hours in front of the hypnotic pictures by Joan Miró. I feel a strange kinship with his disquieting images.

The museum itself is a work of art. The fruity *taches* of Matisse, the mirages of Klee have finally found their home. The walls of the building are slightly concave, and thus the pictures hang without touching the wall, as if hovering in air. The spiral, a symbol of motion, or let us say—of life.

It is an interesting coincidence that they were still building this American museum while I was sketching out some pretty unlikely spiral shapes on my drawing board at the Architectural College in Moscow. The exhibition pavilion I was then planning, as a student, was based on the same principle. Now, as I contemplate this curve, rising up into the sky—not mine, but Wright's—this sense of unity in human imagination fills me with joy.

I am stunned and dazzled by the American dockyards, the markets, overflowing with lobsters and grapefruit, the roads like loud magnetic tapes, full of screams, stridency, music. But in the midst of all this uproar I suddenly shake with—

THE THREE-CORNERED PEAR

I am working on a great theme: the "discovery of America." The poem is based on my American impressions. But in the process of writing, events, life, memories and landscapes of Russia and of the Baltic region intruded on the narrative, diverting the author from the main course of his theme.

Thus, the poem started sinking like an overloaded ship: but at the same time out of it grew an independent organism —the "poem of divagations" which the author now offers to the reader.

ARCHITECTURE:
NEW YORK AIRPORT AT NIGHT

Façade

Self-portrait, alembic of neon: guardian
of the heavenly gates, O airport—
your windows in their aluminum frames
are dusky x-rays of the soul!

The terror,
            of fiery runways & unknown capitals
in the dark sky—

your days and nights, forever sluicing back:
freightloads of stars,
what destinies.

The sea of wings has left pale sediment
of drunkards in your Bar, they're going dim,
like angels,
            snuffing out. . . . Your voice will boom
! ARRIVAL !
            in their ears.

Airfield

Waiting for lovers, heroes, suitcases, miracles . . .
And here they come, five Caravelles
in splendid descent from the stars

five tired streetwalkers of the night, unfolding
their undercarriages so wearily;
but where is the sixth—?

Perhaps she's nothing now—a bird
lost in the sky, a star . . .
cities whirling below,
where is she now,

floating, groaning, gone out of her mind—
a burning cigarette in the fog?

She does not hear the forecasts any more.
The receivers on earth can no longer hear
her messages.

Interior

The forecasts are bad: awaiting the storm
you join the guerrillas in the great lobby.
Fast asleep the Governments lie,
        coupled like careless lovers.
Quietly, like a drugstore assistant
        the control tower assigns them their runways.
The powerful eye, staring away into other worlds.
You are only a fly here,
the window cleaners
slosh water on your head;
you dynamiter of stars, monster compounded of crystals
O it is sweet and enraging to be a son of a future

without fools, or railway stations like wedding cakes—
a future of poets and airports!
Inside the aquarium glass universe the sky lies groaning,
welded tight
                    to the earth.

Structures

The airport: accredited Embassy
        of Ozone & Sunshine!
A hundred generations did not dare
        to tackle this:
the conquest of gravity, supports.
Instead of idols, hewn in stone
        a frozen glass of blue—
                        only, no glass.

Up there, by the ceiling, matter has ceased:
        O edifice of gas!
Brooklyn—stony, idiot world:
The true monument of these times—this airport.

A BEGINNING

Here I am
measuring running discovering
America—in America
and in myself—myself.
Ripping off the peeling skin of the planet
whisking away the dust and rot
digging
        into
              the thing,
descending into the subways:
their lightbulbs are like three-cornered pears—
O show me their naked souls inside!
I won't eat of this fruit, I only want to see
the glassy core light up like an altar
—they lie when they claim the core is an emerald:
cut deeper, it is a watermelon and red, O fiery red!
Be a rodent, persistent
grow lumberman's muscles to get there—
how tough a tough
should the artist be??
Columbus,
don't be a worried cube
blow it by ear
             to the shore . . .
looking for Indies
             you'll get there!

ANOTHER BEGINNING

I am in love
with your burning pillars that rise
up to the stars in the midst of Paradise!
I am a greyhound
stretching out, at long last
a greyhound! And I will catch up with you
and see you plain.
Saw you
galloping through the market
the fast, bare feet
of a beatnik girl. . . .

Under the firehose spouting out endless driveways
my ears were turning like windmills
O godless gasoline poisonous baseball America
Coca-Cola and tolling bells

You, hellish craziness, took me through palace & backyard
my eyes were slamming shut on your women like latches!
I held it out in front of your stores
the showcases clamped their treasures round my neck
but I was looking for Soul I was funky and rude in my
        aqualung
diving down upon Broadway. . . .

The Negro girl, dancing
down in the cellar, a blue flame. . . .
I almost made it but you got away, turning cool.
Read and forgive, I was lost many times;
Gnome-like, I squat on the roof
above the arteries of New York, your sun on my little finger
a ladybird.

STRIP TEASE

Am I yelling?
Or are the kliegs cutting into my eyeballs?

She's tearing off her girdle, her tinsel cloak
hard, yet reluctant: peeling the orange.
Her eyes have the blues of birds, this is a dance
Strip tease: a dance of death.

Bald pates and whistling wolfmouths at the bar
their lushed-up eyes are leeches, full of blood.
One of them is a yolky rockdrill, sweaty, red:
another looks a cockroach, near his death.

Apocalyptic
honk of horn!
With it, I curse you
world of Martian lights on bridges, curse you
love you
prostrate and amazed.

Pouring
herself into the sounds. . . .
"Are you
—America?" I ask her, fool. . . .

She sits down at my table
"O you kiddiecat"—grinds out her cigarette—
"where did you pick up *that* crazy way of talkin'?
Martinis, yes?
                    Or a Pernod, for little me?"

NEGRO VOICE & BONGOS

Homeric drums
and sad sad eyes
we rise like pillars of smoke
we rise. . . .

Refrigerators,
gauze and quarantine—
all that is white is lying down . . .
all that is white is going going dead. . . .

Your hands as pale as chalk
and cold as wax
between the weary shoulder blades
of Negro girls. . . .

Our eyes are dark
in all the markets
for dark meat.

But at night our sweaty sleeping backs
are windows mirroring the stars inside
we, gladiators, negroes, poets, negroes, people
the planets speeding through our own dark skies

the planets speeding through our own dark heaven
when we lie in our beds we are full of legends and
    nebulae. . . .
You won't keep on walking over us for long.
No man can be deaf to the roaring universe!

NEW YORK BIRD

Veering in through the moonlight
an aluminum bird—

it lands on my window sill
fuselage-bodied, its neck metal coils:
and on top, like the flame of a huge lighter—
a face,
a woman's face!

(Wrapped up in his Capitalist bedsheets
my friend lies fast asleep.)
Who are you?
Cybernetics incarnate? A robot?
A ghost? The Lady Day of Flying Saucer Warlords?
Or are you the soul
I was looking for? Weary
and young, a chimera
smoking a Lucky Strike?

Unblinking,
birdlike she sits there, perched, and blue
as gasjets, the pouches below her eyes. . . .
Bird, what good or ill dost thou prophesy?
What is your knowledge? your message?

Now it is rising within me,
the reply—
pipes . . . vessels, intercom . . . the groan of the Nuclear Age
in this room—
        I scream ● and, scalded, my friend
           wakes up and stares at me.

ANTI-WORLDS

The bookkeeper Bukashkin is our neighbor,
his face
        the color of blotting-pads.
But I can see,
burning above him like great balloons—
his anti-worlds! Trembling
under the magical reign of Anti-Bukashkin,
demon, immortal,
sleeping his nights between Lollobrigida breasts. . . .
Yet haunted,
by visions
of blotting-pads.

I greet you,
anti-worlds, true countries of the mind!
Surrounded as you are
by crap and con. . . .
Sages need idiots to right the scales,
oases, deserts; women—
are but anti-men.
Anti-machines stalk roaring through the jungle!
The earth has salt, has shit: but without it
the sun shrivels and is gone!

I love you,
critics: on the neck of one among you
I see a fragrant, naked
anti-head!
. . . I sleep by open windows.
Comets go through space
& skyscrapers hang down like stalactites
grown on the belly of our globe

—and there, head downward
jabbed in like a fork
a happy kid mosquito sits—
my anti-world!

Why do you meet at night
and sit together, staring at TV?
Not listening, but knowing:
it's the first time and the last. . . .
Yet there they sit,
the anti-worlds, forgetting manners, morals
O they'll regret it,
or be made to do so, later!

Their ears are glowing, red
like butterflies they perch. . . .

And only yesterday
he told me, a great lecturer:
"What, anti-worlds?
Such nonsense, my dear boy . . ."

In sleep I turn and toss
at night, in the great beehives of the city
—my cat lies there, his eye is green:
it is receiving messages
                    from everywhere.

GUITAR BREAK

Framed by peppers, bottles of Malaga
Under the fashionable
Backwoods sky
He sits, the young and bony

Singer, riverman: guitar on his knees
Or is it a fiery
Nasturtium?
Shy and bold, a nude

She can chant softly, like a savage
In his secret place
Let the dark city
Hum out of herself

Into silence. Or then, like a roaring
Circus, flip—
A motor bike
In flames

Along the walls . . .! Wild guitars, they are
Our mothers, mistresses,
Costly to love:
Unfaithful,

Amber. Yes, here among the people of the night
He sits, a grim sneer
On his face; cigarettes
Flash to his lips like fuses.

AN EXTORTED DIVAGATION

In America smelling of darkness camellias ammonia
in the hotels of the moon like deer in aluminum forests
panting and huffing like tractors the bloodhounds
seventeen wheezing FBI gullets ahhh-urrr!

One of them with a big shiny tomato head
another a beau, but their boss is humpbacked and sick
in his bloodshot semaphor eye in the hotels
with asses' long ears in the johns where the pisshole
keeps staring at you like the eye of a plaster goddess.

Seventeen cameras clicking seventeen times through the
    crack in the door.
I fly like a gnome through the lens like a bat head down-
    ward.
In hotelrooms on beds or grinning and laughing at sexjokes
seventeen Voznesenskys are in the safes are safe in hell.
Open, their mouths, they look like a forest with arms gone
    numb
like a game of Hands Up that went on too long.

One of them holding water in his cupped hands, he'll never
    drink it!
Another with langouste joys going cold in his teeth.
And one remains hanging mid-air a black chandelier.
Seventeen Voznesenskys are groaning yet voiceless

80

My cries have been torn onto miles of magnetic tape
an endless red tongue, snaked round a big spool
I have been taken apart dismantled and dragged to
      interrogations. . . .
No, I've been back for months, and all alive.

No, I've been back home for months, but not all of me:
somewhere beyond the seas the spies in their spinach-tint
      suits
are watching the movies unwind, with owlish X-ray stares:
there, on the screen, light blue on the couch
you sit, smiling at me, and stretching your arms. . . .

"And he couldn't make it!" one of them grunting
one of them croaking out, "What a chick!"
The hunchback stares somber through one purple eye.
There I am, crucified and transparent, riddled with photo
      bullets
their fingernails, rusty, are trying to scratch at my heart
"Does it hurt Mr. Voznesensky?" Let go let go you creep
      quasimodo
my soul is burning and bleeding, in the glare of Liberty's
      kliegs
the tender wet stares of the bloodhounds—

THEY ARE BEATING A WOMAN

They are beating a woman—
The white gleams
In her eye

It is dark and hot in the car
Her feet
Strike at the ceiling—
Searchlight beams

They're beating a woman
Like a slave

In tears, still beautiful
She rips the handle
Off the door
Escapes by hurtling
Out onto the road—

The brakes
Screamed! They ran across, grabbed her,
Shook her and dragged her and kicked her, face downward
Across a field of nettles,
What a good job you made of it, *stilyaga,*
Childe-Harold, hood—
Your pointed, flatiron shoe
Piercing her ribs:

Such are the joys
Of occupying troopers interrogating the village idiot
Smashing the beauty of the moon!
They are beating a woman
For centuries they've been beating her
Their bells go on tolling
For youth

And live coals
Leave such burning sores
On cheeks. . . .
They're beating a woman

But her soul is a higher flame and not to be snuffed:
Leaving aside all religions, nonexistent signs: there is
The Woman!
         . . . and she lay still, a lake
Her eyes dark waters
Belonging nowhere, to no one
                 like a star
Or a path through the woods

And in the sky
The stars were rapping like rain on a black window
Tumbling down to cool
            her burning face.

BEATNIK'S MONOLOGUE

Go
away, into yourselves, to Haiti, the R.C. church
the lavatories of Egypt, or Egypt, go!
Roaring and miaowing
the human machine at our heels:
"Meat! Human meat!"
The dark machines are our Khans.
At night,
suddenly bold, the robot, cybernetic man
comes sidling up to his creator:
"Give me that woman" he says
"I like them nut-brown
"I love them good, I love them at 30 r.p.m.
"I love them, come on man, give me that woman or else—"
Go!
Up in the mountains and into the beards
into the sea the rivers run dry the fish are dying. . . .
Rolls-Royces are fucking our women,
radiatoractivity. . . .

O you who had plenty soul
chasing through the stone canyons with me

But time made a better sound in fiery Tennessee
where you were a sphinx
light metal your chassis, a sphinx a bird
an old Russian sphinx, with the face and the breasts
of a woman, a wild crazy bird.

MOTOR BIKES: THE HORIZONTAL LIFE

Smiling she zooms in—
To the arena
Her boots lobster red
Her lips a sexy hue:
She flies through the air
A chrysanthemum at her waist—
Amazon, atomic angel, horizontal torpedo!

Their cheeks sag,
Funnel-like: the motor bike
Roars up above their heads, a power-saw—
How dull
The vertical! O Wild One, born
Of Icarus: you know that only squares
And vestals fight
To stay upright. . . .

In this one, billed on posters
Cheered and jeered at
Orbiting beneath the Big Top tent
I see revealed
Their horizontal secrets:
Women, orbits,
Orbits, tears glued back
To the whites
Of her eyes!

She has her Gengis Khan, her tyrant, trainer—
Sin-Hee-Chan: "And don't you think
I have my troubles, too?
What is so great
About her anyway—to stick
To walls, a fly?
And only yesterday
She smashed the camera—
God, all that
Backstage stuff . . . yes, I'll report her
To the Boss; she's bristly
Like a horse thief, too."

But I,
When intermission
Bells are rung, rush to her dressing room
And cry, "O teach me,
Please, the horizontal life!"

But I get no reply
But she just shakes her head,
The amazon. She's still in orbit,
Eyes brimming with
                    such horizontal
                              sadness.

EMIGRE RESTAURANT

They smell of smoky felt,
the creeps!
They are pale like albinos,
drinking my vodka,
munching my pastries. . . .

A small place,
"The Russian Bear."
They said, don't go there.
A little birch tree in a bucket,
all dolled up, yet like a beggar-woman.
At the bar, perched couples
pinned to their stools like butterflies.

Well then, my enemy, creep, dissident
foaming with hate and beer:
whom do you think
you're staring at?
Am I your prosecutor?

For twenty years they have come here,
now they glow
like fireplace screens. And stragglers,
still arriving through the Camps:

"German, and English, North, then South American—
    do you hear, Voznesensky? Do you understand?"
These are the worlds
shook black and blue, the wheels they spin on, gleam
like moons, their foreheads marked by Camps.

    Deafened by jazz, beaten by rain & radiators
    and not a soul left, not a soul. The horror—
    breathing through the vodka:
        "Voznesensky—from which part are you?"
    He sighs, then groans.
    OK.

Behind the window, Martian girls;
and so, their mother . . . ?

But in the twilight on the River Oka
    travels the great pike, in stately silence,
        unattainable: say ssshhh. . . .! And silver, black
            the trousers' legs move through the grass at
                night. . . .
        "The dew! And the grass, so tall, up to your knees:
        O Voznesensky, can't you see?"

Out of the bristly, haggard face
out of the deep swamps beneath the eyelids
    —blue, sudden light:
                    a *man*—
and on his face the forests wave their branches,
rain falls, calves graze:
out of a tunnel roars the train
                    of loss.

And a reflection of birch trees flickers down the cheek,
vertical, weird, and itchy, no doubt—
he doesn't even care to catch it with his tongue. . . .

Opening up
the walls, like Judgment Day
suddenly young and straight—tattoo with searchlights—
"Ma-Ma!"—

         comes the true, hard land
strikes through the frown. . . .

Mosquito-net bonnets on their heads,
old girls,
hung up on caffein.
    "Mike Orlov—what you say? The *Kamarinskaya!*"
Oh, it is weird.
    "Ma-ma!" A sigh, above their heads—
    bongos, accordion: *"Ma-a . . ."*

Once there were Mishas, Mashas, Manyas:
Michaels now, and Maryans—

                  "Ma-a . . ."
And somewhere, in Alabama maybe
they fall on the ground at night,
wanting to eat their way

            back, through—to
            m o t h e r.
With teeth & lips
broken and weary of miracles, countries of shame:
       "Ma-a . . ."
One, from Birmingham, lowing like a calf in the mists—
       "Ma-a-a . . .!"

The lights go dim. We are alone,
but for an old man dozing in the corner—
a Hermit Habakuk, sucking Turkish Delight.

And he, the creep, raises his eyes to meet my stare,
a man. He rises, goes, and out the door
and does not turn.
                    Will he—return?

ON THE METAMORPHOSES BROUGHT
ABOUT BY EMOTION:
THE REBELLION OF EYES

In the third month her laughter sounds strained.
The third month, she wakes up screaming at night.
Above her, like an Aurora Borealis
                    eyes
                        hang flaming in the night!

Her face, lit up in the dim glass
or half her face, like many vertical lakes. . . .

You're getting thin. You don't go to the factory any more.
You listen to them
                    like a gardener from the Moon.
Your life, your pain rise like steam to the skies
    to the bursting pupils of your eyes.
You say, "This blue—I cannot stand it!
    My head will explode!
Someone, ͵omeone greedy, yet stately and strange
    switched on the light in my head and decided to stay
        for ever. . . ."

You are sad: but the eyes are laughing like madmen—
you speak: they're getting ready for a collision.
Instead of tears, these illuminations in your eyes.

"She's only pretending," the neighbors say.
And people pass, like gloomy apartment blocks.
Above her, the eyes go on burning: great windows.
Hundreds of women they carried away, before you.
How much pain they have gathered, to await you!
But once in a century there is a rebellion

of eyes. . . .

Cast out by the seaside, lost and beat
a woman walks, is pregnant with eyes.

Though I have not walked among them,
I have paid for them with my life.

BALLAD OF THE SCAFFOLD

March, 1719

With sagging chins
They crowd the Square,
Good people from Kolomna, Klyazma, come to stare:
"Your mistress
Is a spy! she's in the pay
Of Swedes and Germans,
Greeks and Englishmen . . ."
So she must die.

The Czar:
A fearsome rattle-bones
And black as coal,
His eyes askid like wheels
Of future motor bikes—

And as the head rolls off the blade
Down to his feet
He grabs it, lifts it
For the crowd to see—
It's a red beet. . . .

94

His fingers dig into the cheeks
Like lobster claws
Breaking her nose,
Blood spurting from the neck—
He kisses her.

The Red Square groans,
All dazed. . . .
                    "Aaaaa—aahhhh"
And she replies:
"Great Master, Lover,
Who am I to judge thee?
O thy hands are damp
And taste of salt. . . .
I am a woman, I confess that guilt.
My lips: the frontiers
Of my only Empire.

Such a small love:
Cranberry drop of blood
That trembles in thy mighty beard:
What dost thou care for it? For me—
These days of building
And great fires!

Yet thou hast kissed me
And thy glorious lips
Are covered in my blood,
O generous kiss!
So fragrant—vodka, *borschtsch* & peas. . . .
Such is the love
Thou hast given me.
I am thy slave.
Thy will be done."

The Czar
Stands, petrified
In a black frown:
The melancholy in his eyes
Strikes like a hammer,
Nailing down
The foreign guest and witness.

AUTUMN IN SIGULDA

Time
that I was gone

hanging on to the platform of this train
—good-bye my summer, it is time,
hammers are hitting nails all over the land,
nails to close up the windows
of my shack. . . .

Good-bye my forests, they have shed their treetops,
empty & sad they stand, like accordion cases
the song has gone out of them,
the song—it has left us too,

it is time, to go
it is written
            on the walls, on the faces
of mothers and all women,
an old dedication.
                Good-bye,
                        mother of mine,
at many windows
                you stand

transparent like a cocoon, weary of the day.
Let us sit down a while, let us take leave
my country,
in a proper fashion.
I will become a planet, or a laurel tree
and I am not weeping,
not wearing you out with hard-luck stories:
I say thank you, love, for bearing with me
for a while.

I have tried
               in the shooting-galleries
for 100 points with 10 bullets
but thank you for not letting me make it,

for lighting up my small transparent guns
illuminating them like a red fist
appearing in a rubber glove;

"Andrei Voznesensky"—enough,
no word, no little doggie to be left behind,
nor any "Andryushka" on your burning cheek—

thank you for meeting you in the woods, this Fall
for asking me, I don't remember, what
while the dog was straining at the leash,
thank you,

I had a new shot of life,
thank you for explaining yourself to me,
& the landlady, chasing us out of bed at eight. . . .
On Sundays
we played that growly old record, the songs in hiptalk,
thank you. . . .

But now
you are moving away,
                       as the train is moving away, you are,
leaving my pores, they stand
wide open—we go asunder
you out of me, I out of you;
why can't we make it in this house
                             any more?

You are here, yet you have gone
far way, to Vladivostok almost—

I know, we'll repeat ourselves,
in loves & lovers, in leaves of grass
replaced by this one, by that one—
in nature no space remains empty for long;

so, thank you for the treetops, now blown away,
millions will grow again, thank you for your laws,

but there, she is running—down the slope,
like a burning leaf—after the last car of this train. . . .

Hold her!

SOCCER

Left
      Forward! He's the leanest in the shower,
a record-holder in the way of penalties—
breaks all that crockery, my God!
mind the geraniums, will you?

He's like a bullet among aces
a gleaming parrot set apart from cowards,
he runs, and shoots, and runs:
the Stadium is a magnifying glass to focus
on the smoking ball—

Hissing hoarsely like a hundred syphons
the man who plays right forward toils to cover him
—a hundred medals jingle on his chest,
that is the number of men whose feet
he has undone—

But you
      know, left forward, my lover, how
to use your head!
Good luck to your foes—"Come on, make it *go!*"
Left forward, all your toes!

A thousand eyes
                    and a small Latvian girl
shapely and sweet, a piece
of sun, somewhere among them; O
she hardly dares
                    to breathe. . . .

Attacks, attacks, come, ecstasy! The dizzy joys
of kicking it—the ball, the ball
yet what is in a ball?—but no, go,
                                        go
"Us—Them—God Heaven help us!
What has he done! what has he done!"
The ball,
              in his own goal. . . . He made it, yes
the sun is a black frying-pan.

You walk away,
hunching your shoulders
in the great hush.

Dreams don't come true, the ball
deceives the foot.
The sweet-curved
chick. . . . Oh, her.

You let
the tap splash
water on your head
so full of
blues. . . . And yet,
a murmur:
              "Well, so what—
it *was* a shot! a shot—
                    that's all that matters."

ROCK

The horn

Rock'n it—kick your sandals at the wall!
Rock'n it—down the daiquiri, neon face, your music
shouts & screams—the horn a dancing python snake

or like a herd of cars, all swerving down a dead-end
    street. . . .
Two, really gone ones:
                "Howd'youdo?"

The Ace of Spades—a T-shirt shade, yes blow man blow
that horror horn
           or funnel, to devour

these faces, burlap outfits, wailing parakeets
those two madonnas, real "low-down"—they'll make good
    meat
to grind!

              The spade
                           has hennaed hair: an eclipse
or a clown
               for Judgment Day—
as up on high
                   hangs the umbrella fish, & swings with you. . . .
The Bomb, its parachute!

Rock'n it—beards like torches, bullets instead of balls!
Nothing is straight: the kids in drag, just-married
& the queens—mustaches in burnt cork—
(Hold it! Make a break, revolting Time!)
No, go on
rock'n it! And smash your wristwatch—crash
against the wall!

"That was my watch—now it's in pieces, the old thing. . . .
And barefoot—on the splinters! God, *what* a life. . . ."

Rock'n it—on, on the white floor
(Hey! Watch it! Miss! You'll cut your feet
                      on broken Time!)
                                 but there
they run already
                 rock'n it
across the white and shiny
                        lino floor—
             Blood,
                   blood . . .
                             such crimson tracks . . . !

103

Mix them, shake them!
Crimson cocktails! Let the steam
rise through our shirts,
the kettle is our prehistoric soul. . . .
Fission our mother! We're the compensation
paid our fathers who could never make it,

always lost . . .
So keep your TV sets: we want the furnace!
In the roar of radiators, scooters
we rave through our orgies,

they're like feasts
of death. . . . The Rock, a dance

of doom.

All join in

Great Cannibal, he rules

this land of crystal beauty,
Mr. Mississippi Messiah,

Mr. Rock—
pale like an idiot, with a pork-chop face
Minister, Prophet, Madman—
skyscrapers start the dance

to crush
the ants that walked the streets!

&, *a violin*

To him,
our youth
from the Andes
to the Atlantic,

104

                        neon
                                tears . . .
("Oh no, no, not her, Rock, Rock, she's not yet seventeen!")
                                        dragged on,
moonstruck
                & slow. . . . Rock! Rock!
                                        SOS! Save Our Souls!

CALIFORNIA: THE LENIN SEQUOIA

In California, in the colophony sunsmell
a park of sequoias,
one of them dedicated to him.
"The Lenin Sequoia? Hey—"
O tower of Hell!
"The Lenin Sequoia—"
O great explosions!
Like a red-tongue poodle, his fly unbuttoned
the Sheriff is rushing to see the Mayor.
"Mayor—rebellion—subversion—its roots
pushing and stretching—out all the way now—to Moscow!!"
Help! Help! The Mayor has swallowed his cigar!
He's jumped in the river! Sirens
howling across all America.

The people sit weeping in their underground shelters.
Tanks rumble over their heads in tortoise formation.
The bulldozers charge!
A deep hole is all that is left in the park.
Who planted you, old sequoia?
Who listened to the eternal tree?
The nameplate was melted down, the sequoia is gone.

106

But no: there it is—every day, at high noon
its crown, an enormous parachute! Shining
the mighty beam of its trunk—an illumination!
The sequoia, destroyed, yet there it hangs in the sky!
A secret pall of great leaves above Moscow:
everyone has his sequoia, our conscience is planted!
It is a garden, a guiding light and a friend—
wherever I live, building ship, getting wrecked or just
    having a ball
whenever I am brought down, suicidal—I dive
I dive, the sequoia's silver shadow is my bath of life
and what I am told in its shadow goes beyond words.
There is no sequoia? There is.

END
OF THE THREE-CORNERED
PEAR